**DATE DUE**

| | | | |
|---|---|---|---|
| | | | |
| | | | |
| | | | |
| | | | |
| | | | |
| | | | |
| | | | |
| | | | |
| | | | |
| | | | |
| | | | |
| | | | |
| | | | |
| | | | |
| | | | |
| | | | |
| | | | |
| GAYLORD | | | PRINTED IN U.S.A. |

# OCEANS

Please visit our web site at: **www.garethstevens.com**
**For a free color catalog describing Gareth Stevens Publishing's list of high-quality books and multimedia programs, call 1-800-542-2595 (USA) or 1-800-387-3178 (Canada). Gareth Stevens Publishing's fax: (414) 332-3567.**

**Library of Congress Cataloging-in-Publication Data**

Deep.
    Oceans.
        p. cm. — (Discovery Channel school science: our planet Earth)
        Originally published: Deep. Bethesda, Md.: Discovery Enterprises. © 1999.
        Summary: Explores many mysteries of the ocean, such as the world's highest tides, the life cycle of eels, tsunamis, and the Gulf Stream and Kuroshio currents.
        ISBN 0-8368-3383-X (lib. bdg.)
        1. Oceanography—Juvenile literature. 2. Ocean—Juvenile literature.
    [1. Oceanography. 2. Ocean.] I. Title. II. Series.
    GC21.5.D44    2004
    551.46—dc22                                    2003059202

This edition first published in 2004 by
**Gareth Stevens Publishing**
A World Almanac Education Group Company
330 West Olive Street, Suite 100
Milwaukee, WI  53212  USA

**Writer:** Scott Ingram

**Content Reviewer:** Stephen M. Tomecek

**Editor:** Joellyn M. Ausanka.

**Photographs:** p.12, NASA; p. 14, top left, CORBIS/Kevin Fleming; pp. 14-15, all others, United States Geographical Survey (U.S.G.S.); p. 17, CORBIS; pp.24-25, glass eel © Richard Carlton/Photo Researchers; Sargassum weed © Zig Leszczynski, Animals, Animals/Earth Scenes; p. 28 Sylvia Earle by Natalie Fobes/National Geographic Society.

**Illustration:** pp. 4-5, 26-27, Patricia J. Wynne and Dianne Gaspas; pp. 8, 10-11, 21, Joe LeMonnier; p. 13, Picture Quest; pp. 18-19, Photo Researchers, Inc

This U.S. edition copyright © 2004 by Gareth Stevens, Inc. First published in 1999 as *Deep: The Ocean Files* by Discovery Enterprises, LLC, Bethesda, Maryland. © 1999 by Discovery Communications, Inc.

Further resources for students and educators available at
www.discoveryschool.com

Designed by Bill SMITH STUDIO
Creative Director: Ron Leighton
Designers: Sonia Gauba, Eric Hoffsten, Brian Kobberger, Nick Stone, Jay Jaffe
Production Directors: Paula Radding, Peter Lindstrom
Photo Editor: Justine Price
Art Buyer: Lillie Caporlingua

Gareth Stevens Editor: Betsy Rasmussen
Gareth Stevens Art Director: Tammy Gruenewald
Technical Advisor: Sara Bruening

Acknowledgments: p. 13, excerpts from LOG OF CHRISTOPHER COLUMBUS. © 1987 by Robert H. Fuson. Reprinted by permission of The McGraw-Hill Companies. All rights reserved; p. 19, Aoki and Mooney essays: © 1996 Pacific Tsunami Museum. Http://www.Tsunami@aloha.net; p. 20, excerpt from THE PERFECT STORM by Sebastian Junger. © 1997 by Sebastian Junger. Reprinted by permission of W.W. Norton & Company, Inc.; pp. 22-23, excerpts from ADRIFT. © 1986 by Steven Callahan. Reprinted by permission of Houghton Mifflin Co. All rights reserved; p. 28, Sylvia Earle interview: © American Academy of Achievement. Http://www.achievement.org

# OCEANS

For many thousands of years, people wondered what lay beyond the mysterious horizon where the ocean meets the sky. Once mapmakers popularized explorers' discoveries, attention turned to the mysteries beneath the surface. Although recent technology has allowed the curious and the brave to reach the ocean floor, it is still off limits in places where it drops too deeply. Plenty of mysteries still exist.

In OCEANS, Discovery Channel lets you travel through the vastness of the ocean without leaving your seat. Perhaps your curiosity will make you one of a new generation of ocean scientists.

## Oceans . . . . . . . . . . . . . . . . . . . . . . 4

**At-a-Glance** What if we could take all the water out of the ocean? Some parts would look something like this.

## A Fish Out of Water . . . . . . . . . . . . . . . . . . . . 6

**Q&A** What's the ocean made of, anyway? Who would know better than one of its residents?

## Just the Facts . . . . . . . . . . . . . . . . . . . . . . . 8

**Almanac** Lots of them, from sea to shining sea.

## Water, Water Everywhere . . . Well, Almost . . . . 10

**Map** The world's oceans may all be one big ocean, but knowing the names given to the different parts sure helps you find your way to some amazing landmarks.

## Columbus "Discovers" Something Wonderful . . . 12

**Eyewitness Account** Columbus wasn't the first to sail across the Atlantic, but he was the first to think he had reached Asia. Would he ever be surprised!

## A Little Rough Around the Edges . . . . . . . . . . . . . 14

**Picture This** The seashore—our first encounter with the ocean. But do you know a seastack from a blowhole? Match each picture with its name and description.

## The Tide Turns . . . . . . . . . . . . . . . . . . . . . . . . 16

**Scrapbook** What's the best time to go to the beach, and what does the Moon have to do with it? Why shouldn't you turn your back on the ocean? Where are the world's highest tides?

What's a Tsunami? . . .
See page 18

# Tsunami! . . . . . . . . . . . . . . . . . . . . 18
**Eyewitness Account** Once called a tidal wave, this potentially gigantic killer has nothing to do with the tides. If one is headed your way, watch out!

# Ocean Motion . . . . . . . . . . . . . . . . 20
**Scrapbook** A current is always on the move, but does it really get anywhere? Waves and currents get a lot of mileage, but there's a big difference between them.

# Adrift . . . . . . . . . . . . . . . . . . . . . . . . . . . . 22
**Diary** A modern shipwreck story that rivals the best fiction. Steven Callahan drifted for seventy-six days in the Atlantic Ocean.

# Where Have All the Eels Gone? . . . . . . . . . . . . . . . 24
**Solve-It-Yourself Mystery** Ancient Greeks found it quite believable that eels were the product of mud. No one ever saw them spawn or hatch. Where do you think they come from?

# Down, Down, Down . . . . . . . . . . . . . . . . . . . . . . . . 26
**Virtual Voyage** There are such things as sea "monsters," and they dwell in deep ocean canyons.

# This Woman Dives the Dive . . . 28
**Heroes** Sylvia Earle has gone far deeper than most people.

# Just Skimming the Surface? . . . . . . . . . . . . . . . . . . . . 29
**Careers** Is a life at sea the wave of your future?

# Ocean De-Lites . . . . . . . . . . . . . . 30
**Fun & Fantastic** Sea words for landlubbers, customs, how to name a ship—and more.

# Final Project

## Pass on the Salt . . . . . . . . . . . . . . . . . . 32
**Your World, Your Turn** Can you quench your thirst by building a desalinization plant?

# Oceans

Scientists know more about the surface of the Moon than they know about the ocean floor. It may seem hard to believe, but only 5 percent of the land beneath the ocean has been mapped. All the same, oceanographers—scientists who study oceans—have developed a list of terms to describe the world beneath the waves. We've emptied out the water here so you can really see what's down there.

**OCEAN BASIN**—Area beyond the continental margin, with features similar to those on dry land: mountains, plains, and canyons (known as trenches).

**ABYSSAL PLAIN**—Flat area of the ocean floor that is Earth's most level surface. It is formed when sediment collects over rough parts of the ocean floor.

**GUYOUT**—Flat-topped underwater mountain.

**MID-OCEAN RIDGE**—Earth's longest mountain range, circling the globe from the Arctic Ocean, through the Atlantic Ocean, into the Indian Ocean, and on into the Pacific Ocean.

**HYDROTHERMAL VENT**—Crack in the ocean floor through which sulfurous gases rise from Earth's core, causing ocean water to become super hot.

**TRENCH**—Long, narrow cut with steep sides, in the ocean basin.

**CONTINENTAL MARGIN**—Water-covered area extending from the shoreline to the deep ocean, divided into three regions—shelf, slope, and rise.

**SHORELINE**—Boundary between the land and the ocean, including cliffs, rocks, or beach.

**CONTINENTAL RISE**—Gently sloping area that begins at the end of the slope and extends to the deep ocean.

**SUBMARINE CANYON**—V-shaped underwater canyon cut into the continental slope that resembles a river valley on land. It may be carved out by a turbidity current, probably caused by underwater landslides.

**SEAMOUNT**—Underwater volcanic mountain.

**CONTINENTAL SHELF**—Sloping underwater area bordering a continent and extending offshore from nearly nothing to 1,000 miles (1,609 kilometers) wide and about 600 feet (183 meters) deep.

**LITTORAL ZONE**—Area near the coastline where most ocean life is found, from the surface to a depth of about 600 feet (183 m). Also called the Sunlit Zone because beams of sunlight can be seen to that depth.

**PELAGIC ZONE**—Open ocean water from 600 feet (183 m) to 4,000–6,000 feet (1,219–1,829 m) below the surface. Also called the Twilight Zone, because very little light reaches it. Fewer living creatures are found here.

**BATHYPELAGIC ZONE**—Deepest areas of the ocean, below 6,000 feet (1,829 m). Totally dark. Few living things are found here.

**CONTINENTAL SLOPE**—Steep underwater slope averaging about 12 miles (19 km) wide that drops from the continental shelf to depths as great as 10,000 feet (3,048 m).

5

# A Fish Out of Water

**Q:** We're here today to get the scoop on the ocean from someone whose knowledge goes deep—very deep. Big Fish, how are you feeling today?

**A:** OK, now that the water's back in the ocean. That picture on the last two pages was really weird!

**Q:** Oh, sorry about that. But it WAS just a picture, Big. No one could really take the water out of the ocean. There's too much of it.

**A:** I'll say. It covers 71 percent of Earth's surface. Three hundred twenty-eight million cubic miles, to be exact. That's one billion, three hundred sixty-one million cubic kilometers. Besides, why start moving it now, when it's been around almost forever? And that's no fish story. The first ocean water came from vapor in the atmosphere and water in rocks released during Earth's formation. You don't get much longer ago than that.

**Q:** That's major years back, all right. So when did it all turn blue?

**A:** Never. It's not blue. It just looks that way. See, water absorbs all the red, yellow, and green from sunlight. Blue is the only color of the spectrum left to be reflected by the water molecules. And not every ocean does look blue. Ever heard of the Red Sea?

**Q:** Sure, but I never knew why it was called that.

**A:** How about because it looks red. Red algae changes its surface color. And then there's the Black Sea. The water there has so little oxygen in it that it turns dark. And you've got the Yellow Sea, which gets its color from the yellow mud carried into it from rivers. So what's the next question?

**Q:** Whatever the color, what is the ocean made of?

**A:** Water. Ha! Ha!

**Q:** Very funny, Big. No, seriously. What kind of stuff are you guys hiding in those waves?

**A:** Seriously, there's lots more here than meets the eye. The ocean is like a big wet chemistry lab. The main solids in ocean water are sodium chloride—you call it salt— and calcium carbonate—that's lime to you. And it's got almost every chemical element known, including potassium, manganese—and gold. Only a tiny percentage is gold, but because there's so much ocean, when you add it all up there's enough to give every person in the world nine pounds of the stuff.

**Q:** Wow! We're rich! We're rich! But how do we get it out?

**A:** That's the catch. It's not exactly easy to remove.

**Q:** Oh, well. Easy come, easy go. Next question: Why is the ocean salty?

**A:** Here's a hint: Ever licked a rock?

**Q:** Ugh! No. But what's that got to do with anything?

**A:** Rocks have salt in them. So does soil. That salt gets into the ocean through the water cycle. You know the cycle: Evaporation, condensation, precipitation. Evaporation, condensation, precipitation. Evaporation, condensation, precipitation. Evaporation . . .

**Q:** All right, I get the picture. But I still don't see what salt has to do with the water cycle.

**A:** It's very simple. When the Sun heats Earth's surface, some of the water in rivers, streams, and the ocean evaporates. As the water vapor rises, it gets cold and forms water again. That's condensation. Then it comes down as rain, sleet, hail, or snow. That's precipitation.

**Q:** Yes, Big, I understand the water cycle. Where's the salt?

**A:** I'm getting there. The precipitation falls into rivers and streams, which flow back to the ocean. Along the way, the water picks up minerals from soil and rocks and dumps them into the ocean. When the water cycle begins again, the minerals, including salt, stay behind.

**Q:** So why doesn't the ocean get saltier and saltier? Or does it? Hmm?

**A:** Nope. Most of the salt sinks to the bottom of the ocean and gets trapped in sediment and sand on the ocean floor. But there's still enough left for buoyancy.

**Q:** What's that?

**A:** That's the way a liquid pushes up on an object. The denser, or thicker, a liquid is, the greater its buoyancy. Minerals such as salt increase the density of a liquid, and you know what that means.

**Q:** No, what?

**A:** It means you float better in the ocean than in a pond. The water kind of holds you up. Of course, when you go under, the water pushes you down. It weighs 5.76 pounds (2.6 kilograms) per gallon (4 liters), and it feels like a lot more the deeper down you go because of pressure.

**Q:** How much more?

**A:** At the deepest point in the ocean, the pressure is about 8 tons (7 tonnes) per square inch (6 sq centimeters). That's like a 100-pound (45-kg) human trying to hold up fifty jumbo jets.

**Q:** Heavy-duty! Well, you've really made a big splash, Big Fish. Any last thoughts for us?

**A:** Yep. If all the water were placed on top of the United States, the country would be under 88 miles (142 km) of water. But let's hope that doesn't happen. I want the ocean to stay just where it is. Without it, I'm just a fish out of water. Nothing but a flop.

# Activity

**ATTA BUOY!** How much salt does it take to change water's buoyancy? Measure two cups of water into a bowl. Now float different objects in the water. Use varying materials and sizes: A feather, a marble, a plastic bottle cap, etc. How long do the objects float? Do some sink immediately? Write your observations in a notebook. Now add salt a tablespoon at a time. Using similar objects, note what happens with each addition. How much salt does it take to make a noticeable difference in buoyancy? What is the proportion of salt to water?

# They're All Connected

Two hundred million years ago, when dinosaurs roamed Earth, all the land was connected in one giant supercontinent we have named Pangaea (see right), surrounded by a single enormous ocean. All the ocean water on Earth is still connected—it's just in different places. So for practical purposes, even oceanographers—scientists who study oceans—agree on dividing it into four main parts. Read all about them here, then locate them on the map on pages 10–11.

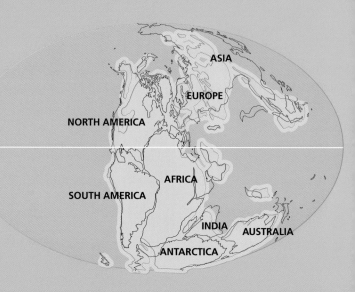

ASIA

EUROPE

NORTH AMERICA

AFRICA

SOUTH AMERICA

INDIA    AUSTRALIA

ANTARCTICA

## ATLANTIC OCEAN

**AREA:** 33,420,000 square miles (86,557,800 sq km), about 9.5 times the size of the United States. Second-largest ocean.

**DEEPEST POINT:** Puerto Rico Trench, about 28,232 feet (8,605 m).

**WEATHER:** Cold, hot, windy. From June to November, hurricanes can form off the coast of Africa and move west to North America.

**CLAIM TO FAME:** Mostly surrounds the world's largest island, Greenland (Kalaallit Nunaat).

## INDIAN OCEAN

**AREA:** 28,350,500 square miles (73,427,795 sq km), about 8 times the size of the United States. Third-largest ocean.

**DEEPEST POINT:** Java Trench, 23,376 feet (7,125 m).

**WEATHER:** Mainly hot. Monsoons and cyclones from October to June.

**CLAIM TO FAME:** Chinese explorers crossed it long before European explorers ventured into the Atlantic.

## ARCTIC OCEAN

**AREA:** 5,105,700 square miles (13,223,763 sq km), about 1.5 times the size of the United States. Smallest ocean.

**DEEPEST POINT:** Fram Basin, about 15,300 feet (4,663 m).

**WEATHER:** Almost completely frozen, with a layer of ice 10 feet (3 m) thick from October to June. No sunlight in the winter months.

**CLAIMS TO FAME:** Ocean floor is 50 percent continental shelf, the most of any ocean. Water is saltier than other oceans because pure water freezes first, leaving the unfrozen part with a higher concentration of salt.

## PACIFIC OCEAN

**AREA:** 64,186,300 square miles (166,242,510 sq km), about 18 times the size of the United States. The largest body of water on Earth, it covers about one-third of Earth's surface, larger than its total land area.

**DEEPEST POINT:** Mariana Trench, 35,840 feet (10,924 m), the lowest known point on Earth.

**WEATHER:** Constant winds keep temperatures between 70 to 80°F (21 to 27°C) near the equator. Monsoons occur from Japan to New Guinea between June and October.

**CLAIM TO FAME:** Contains about 25,000 islands, more than the rest of the world's oceans added together.

## Neptune's Notables— High and Low

▶ The mid-ocean ridge is four times as long as the Andes, the Rockies, and the Himalayas combined.

▶ Most seamounts are found in the Pacific Ocean. The largest seamount is the island of Hawaii, which rises more than 30,000 feet (9144 m) from the ocean floor to its highest peak, Mauna Kea. Although Mount Everest is the tallest mountain entirely above sea level, Hawaii is actually the tallest mountain on the entire planet!

▶ Your every day trench may be about 1,000 feet (300 m) long and 50 to 60 miles (80 to 97 km) wide. But the Mariana Trench in the Pacific Ocean is 35,840 feet (10,924 m) deep, making it the deepest place on Earth's surface. If Mount Everest rose up from the bottom of the trench, there would still be nearly one mile (1.6 km) of water from its peak to the ocean surface.

## What's in a Name

Four names may be enough for the high seas, but closer to shore, people have given additional names to smaller sections of the oceans. Here are some of them:

Sea—Sometimes this means "ocean," as in "deep-sea fishing." Officially, a sea is a body of saltwater smaller than an ocean, with or without an outlet to the ocean.

Gulf—Body of saltwater partly surrounded by land.

Bay—Body of saltwater smaller than a gulf that is also surrounded by land.

Strait—Narrow channel of water connecting two larger bodies of water.

Harbor—Body of water that is sheltered from the open ocean where a port can be built.

## How did the oceans get where they are?

Fairly recently, as discoveries go, most scientists have come to agree on a theory that was laughed at when first proposed early in the twentieth century: The outermost part of Earth consists of more than a dozen separate plates that move on top of a layer of molten rock. Some of the plates are moving toward each other; others are moving apart. It's taken millions of years to make the surface of Earth into the shape it is today—and the plates are moving still.

# Water, Water Everywhere .

North Sea

Baltic Sea
Black Sea

Sea of Okhotsk

Sea of Japan

⚓ 6

Mediterranean Sea

Persian Gulf

East China Sea
South China Sea

Red Sea

⚓ 8

Sea of Oman

Arabian
Sea

Bay of
Bengal

INDIAN
OCEAN

Java Sea

### TOP TEN OCEAN LANDMARKS

1. BERMUDA TRIANGLE—Does this area of the Atlantic between Puerto Rico, Bermuda, and Florida really suck ships and airplanes to their destruction, as the legend tells?

2. SARGASSO SEA—You don't want to tangle with this floating mass of tangled vegetation.

3. SITE OF THE TITANIC SINKING—The most famous icebergs in history!

4. PANAMA CANAL—Opened in 1904, this 31-mile (50-km) canal joined the Atlantic and the Pacific Oceans and saved a trip of thousands of miles (km) around Cape Horn, at the tip of South America.

5. CAPE HORN—This cape, with a combination of strong winds and treacherous coastline, sent many a sailor to an untimely death.

6. STRAIT OF GIBRALTAR—Narrow opening that joins the Mediterranean Sea to the Atlantic Ocean.

7. GREAT BARRIER REEF—This coral reef has one of the richest ecosystems on the planet.

8. MARIANA TRENCH—The deepest spot on the surface of Earth.

9. HAWAII—These islands are really seamounts. When you compute the distance they rise from the ocean floor, its highest mountain, Mauna Kea, becomes the tallest mountain on Earth.

10. BERING STRAIT—Many people believe that until about 12,000 years ago, there was a land bridge here that provided the route for people migrating from Asia to North America.

# Well, Almost

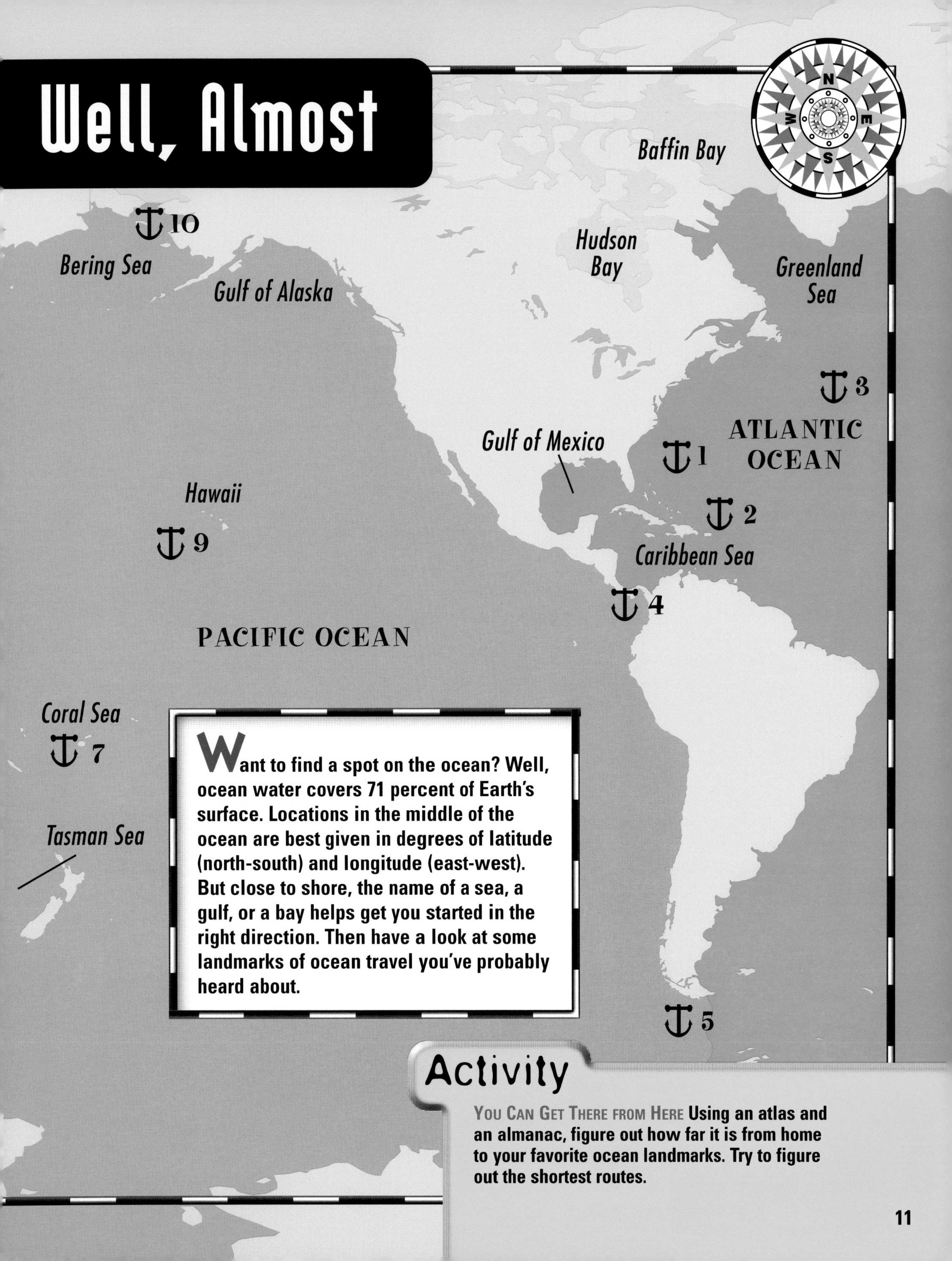

Baffin Bay

⚓ 10
Bering Sea

Gulf of Alaska

Hudson Bay

Greenland Sea

⚓ 3

Gulf of Mexico

⚓ 1

ATLANTIC OCEAN

Hawaii

⚓ 9

⚓ 2

Caribbean Sea

⚓ 4

PACIFIC OCEAN

Coral Sea
⚓ 7

Tasman Sea

**W**ant to find a spot on the ocean? Well, ocean water covers 71 percent of Earth's surface. Locations in the middle of the ocean are best given in degrees of latitude (north-south) and longitude (east-west). But close to shore, the name of a sea, a gulf, or a bay helps get you started in the right direction. Then have a look at some landmarks of ocean travel you've probably heard about.

⚓ 5

## Activity

YOU CAN GET THERE FROM HERE **Using an atlas and an almanac, figure out how far it is from home to your favorite ocean landmarks. Try to figure out the shortest routes.**

# COLUMBUS "DISCOVERS"

One thing the early explorers, ancient fishers, and up-to-the-minute scientists have in common is their realization that the ocean is a force to reckon with. We've learned that we must get it to work with us, rather than try to control it. If you're looking for smooth sailing, the ocean may not be for you. But if it's excitement you crave, there's plenty in store for you.

Although others had crossed the Atlantic and seen the coast of North America before Columbus, he didn't know that. So Columbus certainly had a lot in store for him when he sailed. In fact, he wound up in a place considerably different from the one he expected. Read all about it in excerpts translated from his journal.

## EXPLORERS LEAVE FOR INDIES

**1492 Madrid, Spain**

Three ships—the *Niña*, the *Pinta*, and the *Santa María*—left the port of Palos today on a voyage west. Financed by our own blessed King Ferdinand and Queen Isabella, navigator Christopher Columbus,

originally of Genoa on the Italian coast, is leading a fleet of three ships to the lands of wonder and riches he estimates to be a relatively short distance away. Columbus believes that by sailing west, he will reach the East. This belief is not shared by all here in Madrid. Yet, Columbus has persuaded our king and queen that he will lay the wealth of the Orient at their feet.

NORTH AMERICA

EUROPE

ATLANTIC OCEAN

AFRICA

SOUTH AMERICA

# SOMETHING WONDERFUL

## Excerpts from the Journal of Christopher Columbus

**FRIDAY 3 AUGUST 1492.** We set sail at 8 o'clock in the morning.

**9 SEPTEMBER.** This day we lost sight of land. Many men sighed and wept for fear that they would not see it again for many months. I comforted them with great promises of lands and riches. I decided to count fewer miles than were actually made so sailors might not think themselves as far from Spain as they were.

**20 SEPTEMBER.** Today we saw much weed stretching as far as you can see. This comforted the men since they concluded that it must come from land. At the same time it caused great apprehension because it was so thick it held back ships.

**23 SEPTEMBER.** The crew is grumbling about the wind. The men believe we will never get home.

**25 SEPTEMBER.** At sunset, we saw land about seventy-five miles to the southwest.

**26 SEPTEMBER.** After sunrise I realized that what we saw as land was nothing more than clouds, which often resemble land.

**6 OCTOBER.** This evening, I steered southwest to reach the island of Japan. My decision has not pleased the men. Despite their grumbling, I held fast to the west.

**11 OCTOBER.** The crew spotted reeds and a small board. I now believe that land is about six miles to the west.

**12 OCTOBER.** At dawn we saw people. They are a friendly people who bear no arms except small spears. I showed one my sword, and through ignorance he grabbed it by the blade and cut himself.

**13 OCTOBER.** This island is large and flat. It is green with many trees. It is a pleasure to gaze upon this place because it is so green. In order to save time I want to set sail to see if I can find Japan.

**14 OCTOBER.** I made sail and saw so many islands that I could not decide where to go first.

**17 OCTOBER.** All the people I have seen so far resemble each other. The fish are so unlike ours that it is amazing; some are like dorados of the brightest colors in the world, so bright that anyone would marvel at them. Also, there are whales.

**28 OCTOBER.** At sunrise I approached the coast of Cuba. I am now certain that Cuba is the Indian name for Japan. I have never seen anything so beautiful.

**16 JANUARY 1493.** Three hours before dawn I departed.

**25 JANUARY.** The sailors killed a porpoise and a very large shark. These were necessary because we had nothing to eat except bread, wine, and fruit from the Indies.

**14 FEBRUARY.** The wind increased last night and the waves were frightful coming in opposite directions. They crossed each other and trapped the ship, which could not go forward, and they broke over us. I feel great anxiety because of the two sons I have in school, if I leave them orphaned.

**4 MARCH.** Last night we experienced a terrible storm, and the wind appeared to raise the ship in the air, with water from the sky and lightning in every direction.

**15 MARCH.** I continued my course until I was inside the harbor from which I had departed on 3 August of the past year.

## Activity

**GETTING THE SCOOP** You're a reporter with the *Madrid Messenger*, sitting in the port of Palos and waiting for Columbus's ships to return. Create a front-page story describing the sights and sounds of the crew returning. Interview Columbus himself and perhaps two members of his crew. Remember that they still believed they had found a route to Asia.

# A Little Rough

Have you ever been to the seashore? Then you know how the land changes when you get close to the ocean. In fact, before you can even spot water, there are signs that it's not far away. The plants may change. You may notice sea birds and smell the ocean air.

To people in different places, the shoreline means different things. From the sandy beaches of the eastern seaboard to the rocky cliffs of California to volcanic beaches of Hawaii—and more—coastal features change, depending on the forces of ocean water and weather that strike at them.

A

B

C

D

# Around the Edges

**Can you match the pictures and their descriptions?**

1. Pebbles smoothed and heaped up by the sea (shingle beach).

2. Hole cut through a cliff, then enlarged by the action of the water (arch).

3. Dent in the coast made by ocean water attacking easily eroded rock over time (bay).

4. Flat area of rock fragments finely ground by the sea (sandy beach).

5. Hole worn by waves attacking a weakness in layers of rock (sea cave).

6. Pile of rock rising above the waves that has been cut off from the mainland (seastack).

7. Cliff of hard, resistant rock jutting into the sea (headland).

Answers on page 32.

## Activity

### WHAT GOES AROUND COMES AROUND

People make messes wherever they go, including the beach. With careless littering, intentional dumping, and industrial wastes, pollution is being dumped into our oceans at a fast clip. And when waves and tides wash up on shore, they bring those nasty things back with them. In recent years, many beaches have become unsafe for swimming because of contaminants in the water. Choose a location and find out how the beaches there have been doing lately. Have there been beach closings? Has wildlife been affected? If so, what, if anything, is being done to improve matters? If you don't think everything that could be done is being done, suggest some practical steps that could be taken.

# The Tide Turns

U p and down, up and down, day in, day out. That's the rise and fall of the tides, which we observe at the water's edge. You might think the tides would get seasick. What causes this variation in the waterline, which occurs in most places twice daily?

## YOU ARE THE MOON AND THE SUN TO ME

If Earth could talk, that's what it might say to the tides. Picture this: You have Earth turning on its axis every twenty-four hours all the while it is making its yearly orbit around the Sun. Meanwhile, the Moon is orbiting Earth.

Because the Moon is the closest body in space to Earth, its gravity pulls on Earth. High tide occurs when the Moon is directly above a particular part of the coastline. At the same time, a smaller high tide occurs in the part of the world directly opposite, because the Moon's pull on the opposite side is not as strong. The Moon's orbit around Earth is an oval,

not a circle. So the tide is highest when the Moon is closest.

The Sun, too, has an effect on the tides but much smaller. However, when the Sun, the Moon, and Earth are lined up at the times of the new Moon and the full Moon, there are higher-than-usual tides.

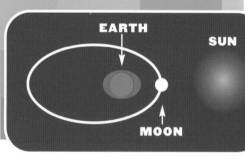

## Living on the Edge

One creature's means of survival becomes another creature's outdoor living museum exhibit. Imagine this: rocky shore, significant difference between high and low tides, an area rich in sea life. At high tide, an area of coastline is swept by waves and fed by the tide of a cool ocean rich in nutrients. At low tide, it becomes a rocky saltwater pool cut off from the ocean. But ocean plants have been growing there, and they make the perfect home for creatures that can survive in this two-part world of the tide pool.

All the animals have found their own ways of adapting to their unusual habitat. Barnacles and anemones attach themselves to rocks and wait for the return of the waves to bring them food. Snails and sea stars clamp down on the rocks to keep from drying out at low tide, but at high tide, they hunt for their food. Sea slugs and tide pool fishes are usually the most active hunters.

If you have access to a tide pool and want to explore it, here are some important pointers:

- Find out ahead of time exactly where the tide pool is.
- Pick up a field guide so you can find out what creatures you might see.
- Explore only at the lowest tides. (You can check this on a tide table.)
- Wear long pants and old sneakers with a good tread.
- Walk softly and don't carry a stick.
- Try to find a pool where at least some of the animals are feeding.
- Decide not to collect sea creatures.
- Watch the ocean for a random huge wave and for the incoming tide.

# Fun in Fundy

**Y**ou have to take tides seriously wherever you are along the seacoast, but especially at the Bay of Fundy, which lies off the coast of eastern Canada between the provinces of New Brunswick and Nova Scotia. The difference between high and low tide there can be as much as 43.5 feet (13.25 m), as high as a four-story building! According to the traditional lore of the Micmac, a people who live in eastern Canada, the awesome tidewaters of the Bay of Fundy were created when a giant whale who angered the god Glooscap made a mighty splash with its enormous tail. Today, scientists believe the bay was created some 350 million years ago, about 100 million years before dinosaurs roamed Earth.

Twice every day, billions of tons (tonnes) of seawater roll in and out of the bay, an amount estimated to be the same as the daily flow of all the freshwater rivers of the world.

Why does this happen? Because of the bay's overall shape and the shape of its bottom, as it narrows and becomes shallower, the water coming in from the ocean has nowhere to go but up. Also, a kind of rocking motion of the water—which happens in all similarly enclosed bodies of water—acts along with the tide.

Because of the enormous exchange of water, the Bay of Fundy is especially rich in nutrients that marine life depends on. Plankton, tiny plants and animals that float on the water, provide food for a large variety of ocean life, from small creatures to some of the enormous whales. The ecosystem of the bay is one of the world's richest, along with the Great Barrier Reef off the coast of Australia and the Brazilian rain forest.

As with any other ecosystem, civilization threatens to destroy the rich life of the bay. Overfishing, pollution, and land development could upset nature's careful balance. The Canadian government has to weigh the immediate needs of the fishing and tourism industries with the long-lasting effects of the practices they spawn.

**New Brunswick**

**Maine**

**Nova Scotia**

**BAY OF FUNDY**

## Activities

**TIE DOWN THOSE TIDES** Tide tables are schedules of high and low tides and are available for many locations around the globe. Pick a spot you like—maybe your hometown, if it is along the coast, or someplace you'd like to go for a seashore vacation.

You can get tide tables from two days to sixteen weeks. Study them and see the patterns. Do high and low tides occur at the same time each day? A number of factors—from the Sun and the Moon's exact locations to the shape of the coastline to waves to weather—make tides hard to predict. But try to figure out when the best time would be for lounging on the beach, for fishing off a pier, for fishing in a small boat, for exploring a tide pool, and for doing other things.

**OCEAN SCRAPBOOK** Make your own ocean scrapbook. Include anything oceanic that interests you, and organize it any way you like.

# TSUNAMI!

**T**sunami is a Japanese word that means "harbor wave." It is in harbors that tsunamis do the most damage. We sometimes call tsunamis tidal waves, though they're not caused by tides. Oceanographers call tsunamis seismic sea waves. Whatever their name, those who have lived through them call them killers.

What actually is a tsunami? It's a wave of water that sometimes follows earthquakes, volcanic eruptions, or underwater landslides. Not all tsunamis are large or destructive. In fact, if you were out to sea, a tsunami could pass under your boat and you would hardly notice. That's because the ocean bottom is so deep. But as the wave gets closer to land, the ocean becomes shallower and begins to cause the wave to crest. Some tsunamis can top 100 feet (30 m) by the time they reach shore. The largest tsunami ever measured was 212 feet (65 m) high.

How fast can tsunamis travel? In deep water, a tsunami can travel as fast as 600 mph (965 kph) per hour. It's important to remember that a tsunami is usually made up of several waves moving together. The distance from the crest of one wave to the crest of another can be as much as 100 miles (161 km). So a large wave could hit, followed an hour or so later by another, and an hour after that by still another.

## THE APRIL FOOL'S TSUNAMI

**M**onday, April 1, 1946, began like most school weeks for teenagers Vivian Aoki and Matilda Mooney. Both girls, who lived in Hilo, Hawaii, near the oceanfront, were hurrying to get themselves and their younger brothers ready for the school bus. Vivian Aoki, eighteen, arrived at school early that morning with her younger brother, James. Matilda Mooney, seventeen, was in her family's apartment with her younger brothers, grandmother, aunt, and uncle.

No one in either family knew that several hours earlier, a huge underwater earthquake had occurred thousands of miles away, off Alaska's Aleutian Islands. About 2:00 A.M., a 115-foot (35-m) wall of water traveling at more than 70 miles (113 km) per hour hit a lighthouse on Umiak Island. The five men in the lighthouse were killed. But the wave did not stop there. It roared across the Pacific, heading for Hilo. In the words of Vivian Aoki and Matilda Mooney, here's what happened.

## VIVIAN AOKI

James and I got to school early that day. There was a park filled with trees near our school that looked out on the ocean, with an open field where a bandstand was built. Behind the bandstand was our school. When a policeman came running into the park and told us to go to higher ground because a tsunami was coming, we laughed. We thought he was playing an April Fool's joke. Suddenly I noticed that the water was moving back from the shoreline and out into the Pacific. I could see the ocean floor. Kids ran to the shore to gather the fish that had been left when the water moved back. Then I looked far out on the water and saw the wave start to build. I screamed that we had to get to high ground.

I ran as fast as I could. My heart was pounding, but I made it to the school grounds. When I looked back at the ocean all I could see was a giant wave. It was like the ocean was falling from the sky. Water rushed at me, covering everything in its path. Children climbed onto the bandstand, but the wave smashed it like twigs. The wave came almost to the school, then it started to swirl around. Children tried to escape, but the wave pulled back to sea, carrying the children with it. I screamed for my little brother, James, but he was nowhere in sight. A short time later, I saw him walking slowly toward school. He was covered with sand and had swallowed water and mud. He told me that he had hung onto a palm tree when the tsunami hit. I took James to the hospital to get the mud and water pumped from his stomach.

## MATILDA MOONEY

My mother had left for work, and I was getting ready for school. Suddenly, the apartment building began to shake violently. The landlord came running up the stairs shouting, "Tsunami! Tsunami!" Behind him, I could see water rushing up the stairs.

I grabbed my two little brothers, but the full force of the wave hit and the building came crashing down. Water covered me, pushing me through the debris. I was washed out of the building through a dark tunnel that had once been a hallway. I was so scared I couldn't even scream. Then my brothers were pulled from my grip.

Out of the tunnel I saw my grandmother and my uncle being washed away. I tried to grab hold of anything that was floating, but the current rushing back to sea kept pulling me down under the water. I saw a little boy holding on to a tall clump of grass. He cried for help, but before I could do anything he was swept away.

I had just about given up. My head was being pulled underwater. Then I felt strong hands grab me and pull me from the water. I was taken to a building to get medical help. My mother was there. I was so bruised and cut that she didn't recognize me. No one else from my family was there. I learned later that day that my uncle had lived. My grandma, my aunt, and my two brothers were never found. That was the worst day of my life.

## Activity

**BRIGHT IDEAS SAVE LIVES** You're a resident of Hilo who has luckily survived the destruction of a tsunami. You're also an inventor. Develop a tsunami early-warning system and apply to the patent office for a patent on your invention. Then write a letter to the editor of the local newspaper, describing your invention and telling how it could be established.

# Ocean Motion

## Wave Hello

*All waves, no matter how large, start as rough spots—cat's paws—on the surface of the water. At winds over six knots, waves start to build. The harder the wind blows, the bigger the waves get. Such waves are called gravity waves. If waves become too steep to support themselves, they start to break. In shallow water, waves break because the bottom slows the waves down. In deep water, the wind builds the waves up so fast they collapse under their own weight. In the case of a boat in a breaking wave, the boat will become part of the curl. It will either be flipped end over end or shoved backward. Pressures of six tons [5 tonnes] per square inch [6 sq cm] have been measured in breaking waves.*

**—From *The Perfect Storm*, by Sebastian Junger**

## Highest Wave Ever Measured:
**112 feet (34 m) by the U.S. Navy Tanker *Ramapo* off the coast of Russia in 1933.**

## WAVE WORDS

**Crest:** Highest point of a wave.

**Trough:** Lowest point of a wave.

**Height:** Vertical distance between the trough and the crest.

**Breaker:** Wave that breaks apart as it approaches land, producing surf.

**Swell:** Large, smooth wave.

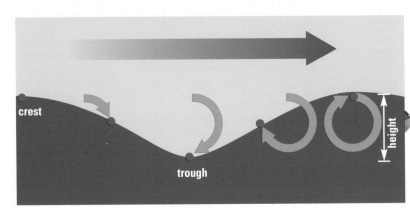

Waves and currents are two additional ways that water moves. Of the two, currents are the long-hard movers, although waves are real shakers.

## Hey, Dude!
### The Killer Waves of Maui

About once a month, storms in the North Pacific send swells south toward the Hawaiian Islands at about 50 mph (80 kph). One island in the chain, Maui, has a huge underwater ridge extending about one-half mile (.8 km) from its north shore. When the swells reach the shallow water, they begin to break. And do they ever break! The speed of the waves is cut to about 25 mph (40 kph). But they also begin to rise to more than 50 feet (15 m) as they approach the shore. It's like skiing down a five-story building. "When you fly down one of these waves, it's not a wave anymore," says one surfer. "It's a mountain moving 25 miles an hour."

# It's Current

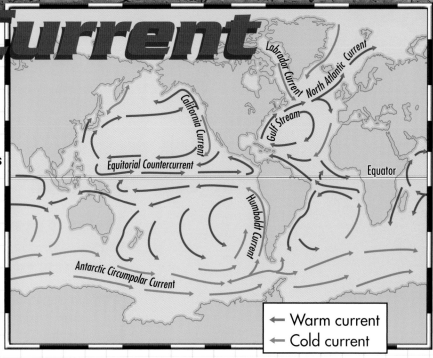

Labrador Current
North Atlantic Current
California Current
Gulf Stream
Equitorial Countercurrent
Equator
Humboldt Current
Antarctic Circumpolar Current

← Warm current
← Cold current

**Current:** A mass of moving water, called a river of the sea. Comes in two kinds: surface and subsurface. Surface currents extend only a few hundred feet below the surface. These currents occur when winds blow across the ocean causing the waters to move. When the surface water moves, deeper water rises to replace it, forming a subsurface current. These currents run deep beneath the surface and at some point turn and flow toward the surface. This is known as upwelling, the movement of cold water from the deep ocean up to shallower depths. Upwelling brings water that contains nutrients called plankton to the surface where fish and other living creatures can feed on them.

## Current Celebrities

### Largest Current

Kuroshio Current, off the eastern coast of Japan, is about 3,300 feet (1,006 m) deep. Because of its dark waters, it is known as the "black current."

### The Gulf Stream

Runs northeast from Florida as far as North Carolina, then flows across the Atlantic as far north as England. Moves 60 miles (97 km) a day and carries 100 times as much water as all of the rivers on Earth. One of the first people to draw a chart of the Gulf Stream was Benjamin Franklin. Warm water from the Gulf Stream reaches the southern coast of Iceland. The water warms Iceland enough so that the average winter temperature of the capital, Reykjavík, is higher than that of New York City.

## El Niño

In a year with normal weather patterns, steady winds blow westward and push warm surface water toward the western Pacific Ocean. In some years, around Christmas time, winds weaken and warm water spreads over almost the entire tropical Pacific Ocean. This warm water prevents the upwelling of cool, nutrient-rich deeper water along the east coast of the Pacific. Fish die and severe climate changes take place. Rain follows the warm water eastward, causing drought in southern Asia and Australia and floods in North and South America.

## La Niña

The reverse of El Niño. At the end of December, westbound winds grow stronger than usual, pushing warm water farther west than normal. This action allows hurricanes crossing the Atlantic to move farther west and to become more powerful than usual.

## Activity

CATCH A WAVE Start collecting interesting tidbits about waves and currents in your own scrapbook. Look for magazine articles, pictures, and memorabilia.

# Adrift

**DIARY**

## Thanks to ocean currents—and his own ingenuity—Steve Callahan survived an ordeal that could easily have killed him.

What would you do if your boat sank in the middle of the Atlantic Ocean? That's the nightmare Steven Callahan faced in February 1982. The boat he built sank in a storm off the coast of Africa. Callahan was left adrift in a 5.5 foot raft he named *Rubber Ducky*. He had a few tools, including a jackknife and a homemade speargun. This is the diary he kept, which was published in the 1986 book *Adrift*.

**DAY 1:** I do not think the Atlantic has emptier waters. I am about 450 miles from the nearest shipping lane. Caribbean islands are the closest landfall, eighteen hundred miles away. Do not think of it. Plan for daylight instead. I have hope if the raft lasts. Will it last? The sea continues to attack. It does not give warning. I open the observation flap and stick out my head. *Solo*'s rudder is clapping, and I am drifting away. The strobe light blinks good-bye. She is lost in the raging sea.

**DAY 2:** Drenched with salt water, my skin has broken out with boils. I'm awakened by pain of salt water burning their tenderness. The raft is too small for me to stretch out in, so I must rest curled up on my side. At least this helps to keep the cuts dry. I am glad to have an emergency kit. In it I have:

▶ A Tupperware box with pencils, paper, mirrors, pocketknife, hooks, and fishing line
▶ Two pints of water in a plastic jug
▶ A bag with food: ten ounces of peanuts, sixteen ounces of baked beans, ten ounces of soaked raisins
▶ One and one-half one-pound cabbages
▶ A sleeping bag
▶ A short spear gun

## Local Sailor Drops Out of Transatlantic Race

Severe weather has halted the Mini Transat Sailboat Race. The race, across the Atlantic Ocean from the Canary Islands to Antigua, was scheduled to begin the last week in January. However, five of the original twenty-five boats have been forced to head back to port due to weather conditions. Steven Callahan of Portland, Maine, has been forced out of the race to repair his boat. He has contacted his parents to inform them that once his craft, the *Napoleon Solo*, has been repaired, he will continue the voyage. He expects the crossing to take thirty days, according to his parents.

**DAY 6:** A shape appears, gliding with incredible speed for the raft. A ten-foot beige body and with a broad hammerhead tells me all I need to know. Maneater. My heart pounds. I hold my spear tightly. I gaze at the shark sliding under me, just below the surface. Making a smooth corner, it circles back, faster now. The beast melts down into the two-mile deep blue as quickly as it came. How often will they come? I will never dare to swim from the raft.

**DAY 11:** Each day passes as an endless age of despair. Everything is soaked. Today, a flat, hot sea surrounds me. There is a great emptiness in my stomach. Fantasies of hot-fudge sundaes dance through my head. Last night I nearly got to taste hot buttered biscuits, but they were snatched away from me when I woke up. Hunger is a witch from whom there is no escape.

**DAY 13:** Quick punches batter the raft. It is not a shark but a dorado. Casually I point the spear gun. Thump. The fish lies stunned in the water. I hoist him aboard. Foam, water, and blood erupt. All my strength goes into keeping the spear tip from ripping into my inflated ship. I fumble with my knife, stick it into his side, find the spine and crack it apart. I cut the flesh into one-inch-square by six-inch long strips. These I poke holes in and thread on fishing line to dry.

**DAY 17:** Things seem to be improving. A shower broke yesterday's heat. I opened my mouth as I did when I was a child trying to catch snowflakes. I trapped six ounces in my Tupperware box. With my knife I peel barnacles from a line. Mixed with rainwater, they made a crunchy soup, which I drank from my box. I couldn't get the idea of a Quarter-Pound McBarnacle Burger out of my mind.

**DAY 27:** As the clouds wander into sunset, I prepare a balanced meal: a few chewy fish sticks which I regard as sausages and a piece of backbone bacon with crunchy flesh. I crack the backbone apart and drop nuggets of fluid from between the vertebrae into my mouth. The real treats are the organs, especially the liver, heart and eyes. The eyes are amazing fluid capsules. My teeth crush out a squirt of fluid, a chewy lens, and a papery thin cornea.

**DAY 30:** *Rubber Ducky* is knocked down again. I haven't slept for two days. My skin is white and even my wrinkles have wrinkles. Fish scales cling to me like slivers of nail polish. What I do not know is that my father is calling the Coast Guard to tell them that I am overdue.

**DAY 40:** I have managed to last forty days, but my water is declining, and I have a few hard pieces of fish. It is also disconcerting to realize that *Rubber Ducky* is guaranteed for forty days of use. If she fails me now, can I get my money back?

**DAY 42:** The sea is as flat and hot as a tin roof in August. My sleeping bag keeps me cool. When I stick my legs under it, they are sandwiched between the wet bag and the damp floor. Nothing to do but try to score some more food. Some good fresh guts should lift my spirits. A big form appears to my left. Humph! Solid hit. I gently pull him toward me. He is food for the week. I lunge to grab him. Too late. His smooth skin slips from my fingers. The big body whirls downward like a bright dead leaf falling from a limb. The waters become black and empty.

**DAY 63:** A dark gray bird swings back and forth, getting closer. I must be getting closer to land. More important, it is a flying lump of food. I shoot out my arm. My fingers close on its straw legs. I twist its head around. There is a silent snap. The meat is of different texture than fish, but tastes the same. Five silvery sardines are in its stomach. I hang them out to dry.

**Incredibly, Steven Callahan survived for seventy-six days until he was rescued in the Caribbean Sea. His ordeal was the longest time ever recorded alone in a life raft and six days longer than Columbus's voyage across the Atlantic a little less than five hundred years earlier.**

## Activity

**LOW-SALT DIET** You've read how Steven Callahan found enough food. But how did he get enough water? Ocean water is too salty for our bodies. Besides collecting rainwater, Callahan made a drinking water evaporation chamber using these objects: a rectangular Tupperware box, a cone-shaped cover for the box, two tin cans, and two pieces of black cloth that fit in the bottom of the cans. Try building your own evaporation chamber, or make a sketch of how you think Callahan collected drinking water from seawater.

# Where have all the eels gone?

Eels! Those snaky-looking, slimy fish that you can find in rivers, lakes, and creeks. There are two common types that have baffled scientists for centuries. *Anguilla anguilla* is found in Europe, and *Anguilla rostrata* is found in eastern North America.

If you've never met an eel face to face, you probably have at least seen a picture of one. Strange things about eels—you can't find fully mature adults, eggs, or newly hatched larvae in freshwater habitats. Why not?

That's a mystery people had tried to solve for thousands of years. Aristotle, the ancient Greek jack-of-all-trades who had an answer—or at least a question—for most everything, thought that eels generated spontaneously in mud. Once people discovered that life didn't spontaneously generate, however, they had to come up with a new theory about the life cycle of eels.

Part of the mystery involves the various life-forms of eels. It wasn't until 1893 that a connection was even made between the larval and adult forms of the species. That's because they look nothing alike. The larva, called a leptocephalus ("slender head"), has a long body shape and large teeth. This contrasts sharply with the adult, which looks like . . . well, a snake.

What does this have to do with the ocean? Well, it turns out that when eels are mature enough to spawn (reproduce), they don't do it on their freshwater home turf. All North American and European eels living in bodies of water that connect to the Atlantic Ocean travel to the Sargasso Sea. That's a section of the Atlantic Ocean northeast of the West Indies that is dominated by a large floating alga, a kelp, called *Sargassum*. But nobody to date has ever caught a mature eel traveling to the spawning ground.

What happens at the spawning ground? A female eel can produce fifteen or twenty million eggs in the Sargasso Sea—and then she dies. The yolk sacs of the eggs break, and the larvae emerge. A year or more later, young eels—called glass eels because of their transparent bodies—suddenly show up at the mouths of rivers in Europe and North America. Only a couple of inches (5 cm) long, they aren't large enough to migrate upstream themselves. Yet later, elvers—as they are known once they acquire body color—are found in the rivers. And eventually, they are growing by leaps and bounds, sometimes far inland.

So how do leptocephali in the Sargasso Sea turn up as glass eels at the mouths of European or North American rivers? How do elvers wind up in the freshwater homes where they spend most of their lives? Can you solve the mystery?

**Answer is on page 32.**

**Use these clues . . .**

- Locate the Sargasso Sea on the main map in this book on page 11 or in an atlas.
- Check out the smaller map on page 21, which deals with water movement.
- Does the location of the Sargasso Sea in relation to the information on this map suggest anything to you?
- In rivers, especially those with wide mouths, seawater is found miles upstream. How do you think it gets there?

# Down, Down, Down

Thousands of miles (km) across the Pacific Ocean is New Zealand, made up of two large islands, North Island and South Island. On the northeast coast of South Island is a mountainous peninsula the Maori people named Kaikoura (KIGH koor uh).

It was formed 125,000 years ago by the volcanic action of plates beneath the waters offshore. That action also formed the destination for your virtual voyage: Kaikoura Canyon. Just beyond the shore, the bottom drops to 2,600 feet (792 m), then plunges to the canyon bottom more than one mile (1.6 km) below. It's the start of a seafloor channel 1,000 miles (1,609 km) long. Kaikoura is not the deepest spot in the ocean, but it's quite a trip.

Upwelling currents from the blackness of the mile-deep (1.6 km) canyon bring cold water rich in nutrients toward the surface. The waters are filled with sea life, including sperm whales and giant squid, one of the rarest creatures on the planet.

**The Dive** The great thing about this trip is that you don't need to swim or even breathe underwater. All you have to bring along is your imagination. As you slip beneath the waves, it's as if you're on the ceiling of an enormous room, so large that you can't see the floor. As you descend the first 100 feet (30 m), notice those reddish clouds. They're krill, tiny shrimplike creatures that are an important food source for a wide variety of sea creatures, including whales. Krill are drawn toward the surface by the upwelling current.

Watch out! That mako shark is looking for a snack. It doesn't eat krill, but it does eat other krill eaters, such as the octopus. Most sharks are harmless, but the mako and the blue have been known to attack humans, so maybe you'd better scurry along. Those sharks can't follow more than a few hundred feet (91 m).

You're now 700 feet (more than 213 m) down. That thing over there that looks like a mountain? It *is* a mountain, called a seamount. It rises from the floor of the canyon to a height of 4,600 feet (1,402 m).

A school of albacore tuna swims by. Those small pink fish that look like sunfish are called orange roughies.

**On Top of a Mountain** Let's wait here until we see . . . Wow! Look at the size of that whale! See the long, narrow mouth on the underside? It's a sperm whale, one of the few toothed whales. Awesome, isn't it? Sperm whales can grow 60 feet (18 m) long and weigh more than 50 tons (45 tonnes). They eat a ton of food a day. They can dive one mile (1.6 km) deep and stay underwater for several hours. How about following this big fellow?

**In the Dark** It's a good thing you can see in the dark—because it is pitch black here. Faint rays of sunlight reach only 2,000 feet (610 m) below the surface. A lot of the creatures down here are bioluminescent—they can make their own light, like fireflies. Look at those eels and those long-bodied tadpole-shaped fish, which are called ling. Don't worry about these sharks—they're harmless species: spiny dogfish and plunket.

**Smooth Landing** Feel that fine sand on the canyon floor? It's called silt. It's been shaken loose from canyon walls and seamounts during undersea earthquakes. Ah, both you and the sperm whale have gone about as far as you can go. You see him, but he doesn't see you. See the round, ragged scars on his snout? They were made by the suckers on the tentacles of giant squid. The whale has probably seen many battles with squid.

Wouldn't it be great to see one of those giants? If you did, you'd be the first human to see one alive. They are much like their tiny cousins who live in shallower depths, except that they can grow up to 60 feet (18 m) long and weigh up to one ton. Their boneless bodies are covered with a rubbery skin. The head is connected to a band of muscle, which leads to eight tentacles as thick as fire hoses. Two longer, thinner tentacles extend beyond those eight. At the end of the tentacles are four rows of suckers that look like mouths with tiny pointed teeth.

To capture a prey, perhaps a barracuda or a shark, the squid shoots out its tentacles like bungee cord. It pulls the catch back to its parrotlike beak and cuts the flesh into bite-sized chunks. The food slides down the squid's throat, past its brain, to its stomach. If the squid takes too big a bite, it could suffer brain damage!

**Fight!** In this darkness, it's no surprise that the giant squid has the largest eyes of any animal—as big as your head. All the better to see you . . .uh, oh. Is it coming after you? No! You're about to be the first human to witness a battle between a sperm whale and a giant squid. The whale is the squid's only natural enemy. These two sea creatures are at the top of the food chain that began with the krill you saw thousands of feet above.

What a battle! It looks like the whale has won—he's swallowing the squid. It's probably time for him—and you—to head toward the surface. Now, don't go up too quickly.

# Activity

**LET'S GO TO THE VIDEOTAPE** You're a sports announcer covering the blow-by-blow struggle between the sperm whale and the giant squid. Write the scene as though you're ringside at the bottom of Kaikoura Canyon.

# This Woman Dives the Dive

Sylvia Earle may not be as well-known an ocean explorer as Jacques Cousteau, but in her own way, she has done as much for the oceans of the world. Earle has spent more than six thousand hours underwater and has photographed or documented more than twenty thousand marine plants. In 1970, Earle and four other women lived for two weeks underwater. Nine years later, she completed the deepest unconnected human dive in history—1,250 feet (381 m). Wearing a special suit to withstand the pressure of 600 pounds (272 kg) per square inch (6 sq cm), Earle spent more than two hours exploring the deep ocean. In this interview, she talks about the world's oceans, and their importance in her life and in all of our lives.

### Q: When did you become interested in the ocean and sea life?

When I was a child my family used to go to the New Jersey shore for vacations. We didn't live near the beach, but it wasn't that far away. New Jersey is a relatively small state; nothing is very far from anything else. I think in my earliest years, the ocean became special because it wasn't there all the time, I never took it for granted. I didn't exactly worship the ocean, but I really regarded it as a very special opportunity. I can remember as we came to the sand dunes along the shore, before we could see or hear the ocean, we could smell it. And then hear it. And then finally, there it was, this great expanse. I can still feel that leap of joy at finally getting out to the beach and running around.

### Q: What about marine biology? When did it occur to you that that's what you wanted to do?

When I was twelve, my parents moved from New Jersey to Florida. We lived right on the water. The Gulf of Mexico became my back yard. Instead of going out to climb trees, I had the pleasure of getting acquainted with salt marshes, and sea grass beds, which were populated with things such as sea horses and sea urchins, and great crabs with long, spindly legs. You never knew what you were going to find just walking around in these squishy, beautiful, clear water areas. That used to be a place that lived up to its name—Clearwater. At the time I was a child it had clear water. It isn't that way anymore. But I was fascinated by wild creatures. The decision to focus on marine science took a while. When I was still a student at Florida State University, I began my lifetime project to explore the plants in the Gulf of Mexico.

### Q: What was your first dive like?

The first real dive in the ocean, aside from splashing around as a youngster with a face plate, was using a scuba tank at Florida State University when I was taking a summer course. For almost two months, we had a chance to get to know who lives in the ocean and what it all means. This was in 1953. The professor had two of the first scuba tanks in the country. We went out in a little boat, where the water was 15 feet [5 m] deep. Each of us had a few minutes of instruction. I remember the most important words were "Breathe naturally. Don't hold your breath. Put the regulator in your mouth, and don't stop breathing." This was before there were handy guides on scuba diving, before there was a lot of the understanding about how quickly you can get into trouble breathing compressed air and holding your breath or coming up too fast. This was my first experience in having the sensation of breathing under the water and feeling free, being thrown over the side, and feeling that I'm underwater and I can breathe. I was so impressed that I could stay there and didn't have to go back up after thirty seconds or so. I could just watch these little creatures. And engage them, and let them engage me. I could stand on one finger! And do back-flips! I was awed by this new ability to be able to meaning-fully engage the creatures there. I had to be dragged out of the water!

**Q: You've been called Her Deepness rather than Her Highness because of your concern about the world's oceans. What's the warning cry that you would like to sound?**

My message is simple: If the sea is sick, we are sick; if it dies, we die. Our future and the state of the oceans are one. Without oceans, the planet would not be hospitable for us. The oceans drive the climate and create the atmosphere. We assume things have always been this way, and they always will be this way. Scientists who are looking at other places in the universe, where life may occur, look first for the existence of water. There's nothing like the diversity of life in the sea.

# Just Skimming the Surface?

Does Sylvia Earle's career sound like the career for you? Do you think you might become an oceanographer someday? Along with an intense curiosity about the ocean and how it works, you'll need an undergraduate degree in a basic science such as biology or geology. Most ocean scientists hold a graduate degree in oceanography as well. Why not start preparing now? In middle school or junior high and high school, sign up for science and math courses, and check out related subjects such as geography. And don't overlook computer and writing classes—you'll need them for observing phenomena, analyzing data, and writing research papers.

Sound like a lot of hard work? Well, it is, but if you love it, your career can take off in different directions. Usually a large project requires ocean scientists with different specialties. For example, if you're not up (or down) for undersea exploration, you can work in a lab doing crucial research on ocean events such as El Niño. Or maybe you'll enter ocean engineering, a related field that encompasses designing structures, equipment, and experimental studies. Or maybe you'll be an ocean technician, responsible for maintaining equipment, doing measurements, and data processing. Generally, you need only a two- or four-year degree for this.

Whatever you do in the field of oceanography, however, you can be sure you'll be helping to make our planet a better place.

The ocean has contributed a whale of a lot to the language we speak. Even though you may have been using phrases such as *all in the same boat, navy blue, small fry,* or *go off the deep end,* you may not have gotten the drift about some words that possibly first came from the deep briny. Here are some of them.

**Groggy** comes from grog, the name sailors in the British Navy used for their daily ration of a half-pint of rum. Before drinking, sailors would toast each other by saying "down the hatch."

**Overwhelm** comes from an old English word meaning "to capsize."

**First-rate** comes from the system used for hundreds of years in the British Navy to evaluate its warships.

**Stranded** comes from *strand,* an old English word for beach, which is where boats that sailed into shallow waters ended up.

**Rummage sale** comes from the French word "arrimage," meaning "the loading of a cargo ship." Damaged goods were sometimes sold at large warehouse sales.

**Okay** comes from the French too. Cargo that was safely unloaded was said to be "au quay" (on the quay) or—as we know it—the dock.

**Skyscraper** was the sailor's term for the tallest sail on the ship, the topsail.

**Slush funds** were once the personal funds of the ship's cook, who earned them by skimming off the fat, or "slush," from cooking and selling it in port.

**Gung ho** is from the Chinese sailors, who would encourage one another to gung ho or "work together" to accomplish shipboard tasks.

**Denim jeans.** You won't believe this one! Italian sailors were fond of pants made from a sturdy cloth woven in Nimes, France. The cloth was said to be "from Nimes." The Italian sailors who wore the pants were mainly from the port city of Genoa. Those sailors were known as Gens. Thus, we have Gens wearing pants made of de Nimes.

**Nausea,** that upset queasy feeling in one's stomach, comes from the Greek word *naus,* meaning ship.

**Posh,** a word meaning fashionable or expensive, originated on the docks of Boston. The trunks of wealthy travelers would carry the label POSH, which stood for "portside out, starboard home." Those were the sides of the ship where luggage was to be kept to avoid damage from sun, salt, and water.

# WHeN at Sea . . .

▶ Scottish law once required fishermen to wear a gold earring, which was used to pay for funeral expenses if they drowned and washed ashore.

▶ Legend has it that an umbrella aboard ship is unlucky.

▶ In the early days of the British Navy, cannons were fired from warships as a greeting. Since the cannons could not be quickly reloaded, firing a gun in salute told receivers of the greeting that the firers had disarmed themselves and could do no harm. The largest ships of the fleet had twenty-one guns on each side, so a twenty-one gun salute was a sign of the greatest respect.

▶ "What the sea wants, the sea will have," was a saying in the British Isles. This meant that if a sailor was meant to drown, nothing could prevent it. Thus, few sailors of the past ever learned to swim.

The words that follow are in some way all connected with the sea. See if you can figure out where they came from.

ASTRONAUT—a person trained to make spaceflights.

STRIKE—a refusal to work.

ABUNDANCE—a great supply.

LISTLESS—having no interest in what is happening.

SALARY—an amount of money paid at regular times.

**Bonus question.** What was keelhauling?

## The Lengths That Some People Will Go To

In 1947, Thor Heyerdahl attempted to prove that ancient South Americans had sailed across the Pacific Ocean to settle islands in Polynesia. On the *Kon-Tiki*, a raft made of balsa wood, Heyerdahl and a small crew sailed more than 4,200 miles (6,758 km) in 101 days from Peru to Fiji.

# What's in a Name?

During World War II, the United States Navy began this system for naming ships:

▶ *Battleships* after states of the Union.

▶ *Destroyers* in honor of dead persons associated with the Navy or Marines.

▶ *Submarines* after fish or other sea life.

▶ *Hospital ships* with words synonymous with kindness.

▶ *Storage ships* after astronomical bodies.

**So . . . what kind of craft is the**

U.S.S. *Mercy?*　　U.S.S. *John F. Kennedy?*

U.S.S. *Nautilus?*　　U.S.S. *Neptune?*

U.S.S. *Missouri?*

**Between 1825 and 1834, Lieutenant Matthew Fontaine Maury of the U.S. Navy made three long ocean voyages—to Europe, to the Pacific Coast of South America, and around the world. He was the first person to systematically study oceans, and he did it as his full-time job, too! In 1855, *The Physical Geography of the Sea*, considered the first book on oceanography, was published.**

# DEEP-SEA GROANERS

**What did the Atlantic Ocean say to the Pacific Ocean when they met?**

Nothing. It just waved.

**Why is Christmas coming early this year?**

Because the cat went to the beach and came back with sandy claws.

**How did the captain want the deck to look?**

Shipshape.

**How many feet below sea level is the Mariana Trench?**

Now that's a deep question!

**What kind of soap keeps you afloat?**

Lifebuoy.

**Why didn't the fish go to the movies on Saturday?**

They preferred to stay in school.

**Why couldn't the flounder join the chorus?**

Because it sang flat.

**What was the ocean's favorite subject in school?**

Current events.

**What did the ship say to the pier?**

What's up, dock?

## Salt of the Earth

The oceans are not the saltiest bodies of water on Earth. The Dead Sea, in Israel, and the Great Salt Lake, in Utah, are saltier. It's also easier to float in them, because the increased salt content makes them denser.

**Thar She Blows!** In recent years, that cry less likely comes from a whaling ship's captain than from a worker on an offshore oil rig. Yes, there's oil, also called petroleum, under some ocean water. People got the idea to drill for it by understanding how it was formed from decayed once-living things that "cooked" in Earth's heat. The places where oil is found today under dry land were once under water. So it makes sense that oil also lies underneath nearby coastal waters.

All answers on page 32.

# Final Project:
# Pass on the Salt

**D**esalinization is the process of removing salt from water. How would you desalinate enough ocean water to supply the needs of a desert city or country that is near an ocean?

Rain is another source of water. Of course it doesn't rain often in the desert. But suppose you could build a large container that allowed you to create your own storm? Let's call it the storm tower and let's say it's the shape of a cylinder. Once you get the concept, you can worry about size. What you need to figure out is how to create a cool upper atmosphere.

The next problem is that the process of evaporation works slowly. It took Callahan hours just to get a few pints of water. How would you make evaporation happen faster? Well, did you know that a rotor spinning at a speed of 100 mph (161 kph) can create a swirling effect similar to that of a tropical storm or hurricane?

## OK, it's time for you to take over:

Create a plan using the information above to build a desalinization plant. Imagine that pipes, a pump, metal, rotors, and anything else you need are right at your fingertips. And remember this: *Warm, wet air circulates down.*

## ANSWERS

**Picture This pages 14–15:**
1. B   2. A   3. G   4. C   5. F   6. E   7. D

**Solve-It-Yourself Mystery, page 24:**
If you compare the location of the Sargasso Sea with the map of ocean currents, you'll notice that the Gulf Stream passes through the area. The Gulf Stream is a major Atlantic Ocean current that brings warm water north, close to the Atlantic Coast of the southern United States, then turns northeast and heads toward Europe. The leptocephali are carried on the Gulf Stream. The North American version probably exits the Gulf Stream earlier, while the European version stays for the ride on the North Atlantic current, an extension of the Gulf Stream.

The glass eels that survive the long, perilous journey and find themselves at the mouth of rivers are not large enough to swim upriver themselves. They rely on the incoming tide. Once they are at home in the river, the elvers are able to swim some, rest in the bottom mud, then continue swimming. After a number of years, they are ready to return to the Sargasso Sea.

**Fun & Fantastic Quiz, page 30:**
Bonus question: to "keelhaul" someone means to severely punish; What's in a Name? U.S.S. Mercy: hospital ship, U.S.S. Nautilus: submarine, U.S.S. Missouri: battleship, U.S.S. John F. Kennedy: destroyer, U.S.S. Neptune: storage ship.